Contents

Ordering	1	Pascal's triangle	24
Tombola	2	Waiter worries	25
Lighthouses	3	Fraction grid	26
Birthday bill	4	Fractions	27
Souvenirs	5	Triangles	28
Car dealer	6	Problems	29
Fractions	7	Space stations	30
Walk graph	8	Building a den	31
Mean, median and range	9	Brain teasers	32
Conversion graph	10	Probability	33
Angles	11	Birthday puzzle	34
Recipe book	12	School survey	35
Space travel	13	Labyrinth	36
Map	14	Number clouds	37
Jackpot	15	Phone bill	38
Housemates	16	Cycle race	39
Factors	17	Mystery angles	40
Prime addition	18	Triangles	41
Card addition	19	Temperature and weight	42
Superbrain	20	Sports shops	43
Rockets	21	Flower power	44
Problems	22	Factors	45
Gardens	23	Code squares	46

About this book

Most of the work in this book is for you to do on your own.

Sometimes you will work with a friend.

You will need instructions from your teacher to do some of the work.

Sometimes you need things to help you. The pictures at the bottom of each page show you what you need.

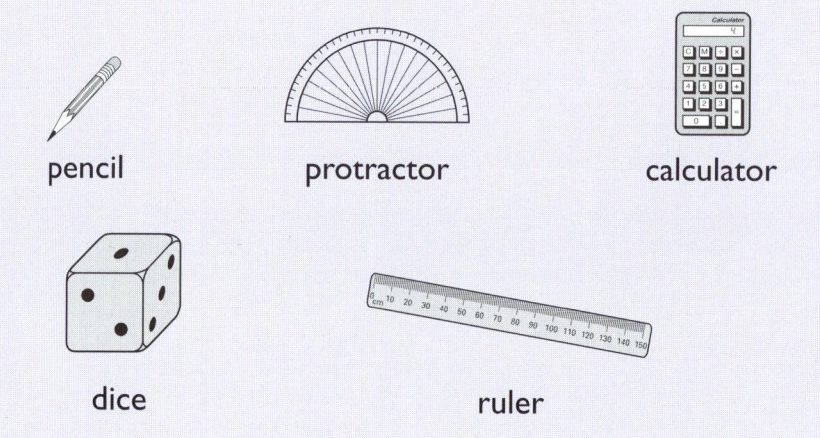

pencil

protractor

calculator

dice

ruler

At the bottom of some pages, there is extra work your teacher might ask you to do. It has a key next to it, like this:

Work carefully! Read each question all the way through before trying to work out the answer.

Do not write in this book.

Ordering

Write three numbers which lie between each pair.

1. 0·4 and 0·6
2. 0·2 and 0·7
3. 0·1 and 0·2
4. 0·25 and 0·35
5. 0·04 and 0·07
6. 0·15 and 0·4
7. 0·09 and 0·08
8. 0·92 and 0·89

Write the number which lies halfway between each pair.

9. ⁻7 and 1
10. 6 and 9·4
11. ⁻49 and ⁻13
12. 0·04 and 0·34
13. 0·01 and 0·17
14. ⁻73 and 29
15. 0·6 and 0·9
16. ⁻4 and 37
17. ⁻19 and 58
18. 0·015 and 0·065

Write the value of the digit 7 in each number.

19. 5·07
20. 79·63
21. 3·764
22. 25·7
23. 731·92
24. 39·007
25. ⁻79
26. 0·72

Write some pairs for your friends to find the 'halfway' numbers.

Tombola

Write the tombola tickets which win each type of prize.

Multiples of **3, 5 and 7** win a computer game.

Multiples of **3 and 5**, **but not of 7**, win a cuddly toy.

Multiples of **5 and 7**, **but not of 3**, win a board game.

Multiples of **3 and 7**, **but not of 5**, win a football.

Tickets which are **not** a multiple of **3, 5 or 7**, win a lollipop.

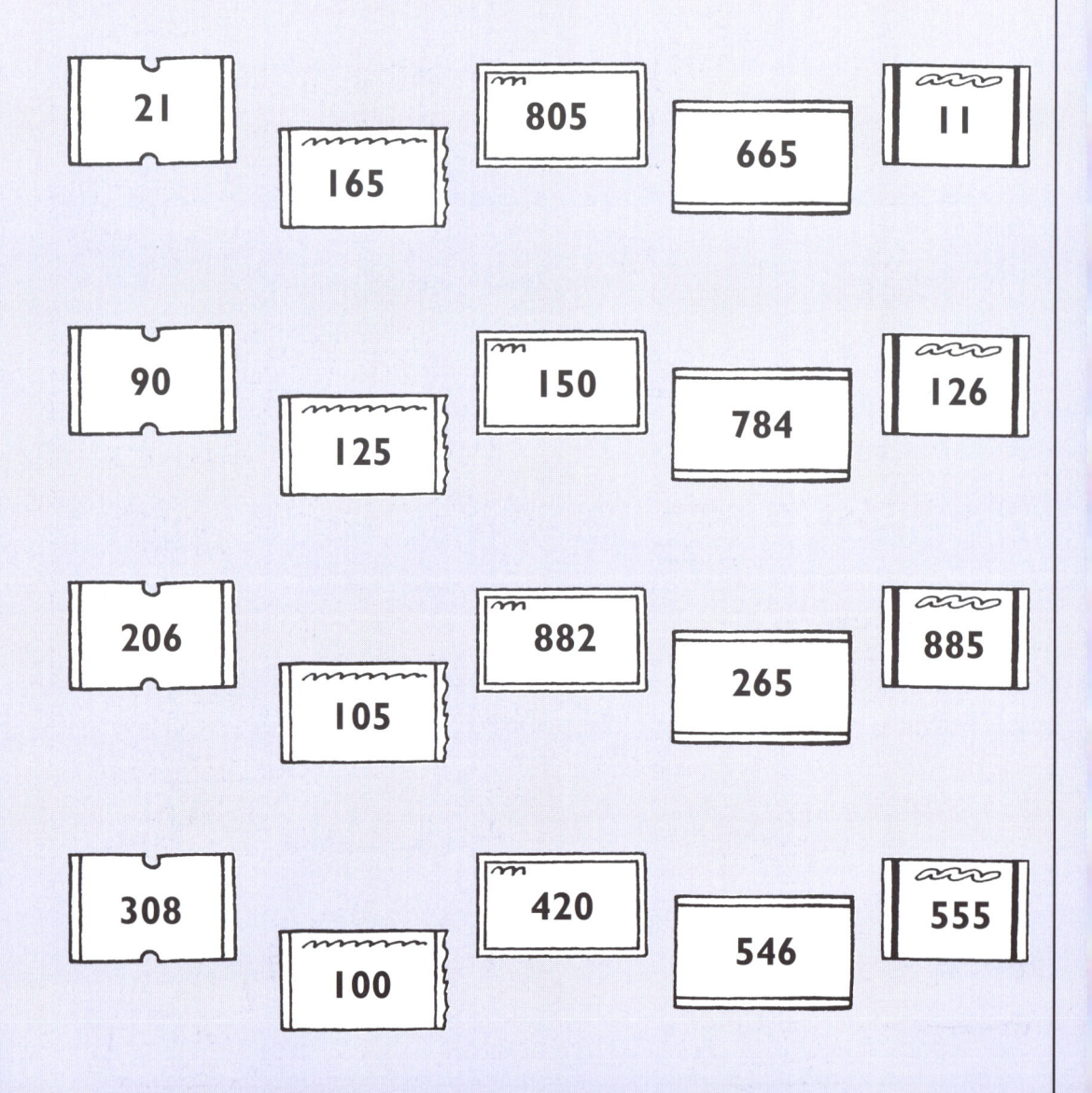

21   165   805   665   11

90   125   150   784   126

206   105   882   265   885

308   100   420   546   555

Pick a ticket and write all its factors

Lighthouses

Write multiplications and divisions using the boat and lighthouse numbers.

1. Lighthouse: 58, 169, 359, 1224 — Boat: × 6

2. Lighthouse: 360, 1248, 3824, 10240 — Boat: ÷ 8

3. Boat: ÷ 9 — Lighthouse: 1872, 594, 7758, 2367

4. Boat: ÷ 11 — Lighthouse: 6710, 9680, 4510, 2189

5. Lighthouse: 372, 683, 2416, 3270 — Boat: × 12

6. Lighthouse: 4560, 2321, 1734, 991 — Boat: × 11

7. Boat: × 9 — Lighthouse: 452, 7681, 1041, 2324

8. Boat: × 7 — Lighthouse: 777, 8214, 2613, 1524

9. Boat: ÷ 7 — Lighthouse: 4907, 6377, 2541, 4557

10. Boat: ÷ 12 — Lighthouse: 2832, 3720, 12648, 36012

3

Birthday bill

Rosie goes to a café on her birthday.

This is the bill:

Cheese and tomato pizza	£3·75
Burger and chips	£4·00
Chicken sandwich	£3·80
Pasta	£5·00
Salad	£2·00
Pancakes	£1·50
Ice cream	£2·25
Big birthday cake	£6·00
Drinks	£8·00

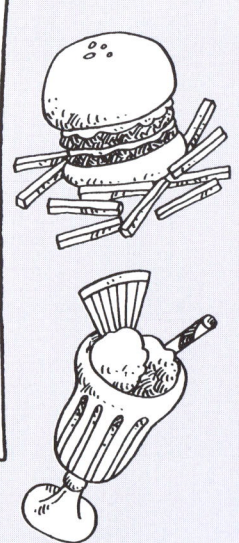

Rosie's penfriends ask her how much things cost in Britain. Convert the price of each item on the bill for each penfriend. Give your answers to two decimal places.

Rosie writes to:

1. Woorin in Australia
2. Tsing Mai in Hong Kong
3. Gudmund in Iceland
4. Katya in Russia
5. Yuki in Japan
6. Rajit in Bangladesh

Exchange rates

£1 =

A$2·59 Australian dollars

HK$12·69 Hong Kong dollars

IKr113·31 Icelandic Krona

R36·8 Russian Rubles

¥185·75 Japanese Yen

Tk79·21 Bangladeshi Taka

Find out the exchange rate for another currency and convert a bill of your own.

Souvenirs

t-shirt £6·50
keyring £1·60
biscuits £3·70
jigsaw £4·45
poster £2·40
jumper £8·25
teapot £5·65

Work out how much each person spends and convert the total into their own currency.

£1 =

S$ 2·76 Singapore Dollars

R 10·02 South African Rand

Rs 83·3 Pakistani Rupees

NZ$ 3·03 New Zealand Dollars

Can$ 2·15 Canadian Dollars

5·87 Israeli New Shekel

1. Tim from South Africa buys a teapot, two posters, a jigsaw and a keyring.
2. Rana from Israel buys a jumper, a poster, three boxes of biscuits and a jigsaw.
3. Mike from Singapore buys two t-shirts, a box of biscuits, a jumper and three keyrings.
4. Hema from New Zealand buys a teapot, a poster, two jigsaws and a keyring.
5. Aslam from Pakistan buys four jumpers, two teapots and two posters.
6. Pierre from Canada buys three jumpers, four keyrings and three jigsaws.
7. Bart from Israel buys a jumper, a box of biscuits, three posters and a t-shirt.
8. Tiki from South Africa buys two boxes of biscuits, a jumper and three keyrings.
9. Sue from Singapore buys a poster, a jumper and four jigsaws.
10. Jamila from Pakistan buys two t-shirts, two jumpers and two jigsaws.
11. Louise from Canada buys two keyrings, three jigsaws and three teapots.
12. Sam from New Zealand buys four boxes of biscuits, three t-shirts and six keyrings.

Car dealer

Carla the car dealer sells second-hand cars. She buys them for 38% less than their price when new.

She sells them for 26% more than she paid for them.

How much profit will Carla make on each car?

1. Price when new
   £9800

2. Price when new
   £12 000

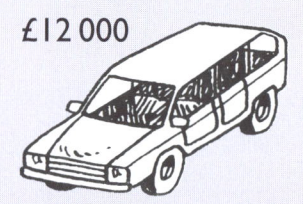

3. Price when new
   £5650

4. Price when new
   £14 700

5. Price when new
   £8900

6. Price when new
   £24 600

7. Price when new
   £19 800

8. Price when new
   £11 200

Would Carla sell the cars for more or less if she decided to:

9. buy the cars for 42% less than their price when new, and sell them for 30% more than she paid for them?

10. buy the cars for 16% less than their price when new, and sell them for 9% more than she paid for them?

11. buy the cars for 28% less than their price when new, and sell them for 22% more than she paid for them?

12. buy the cars for 52% less than their price when new, and sell them for 37% more then she paid for them?

Fractions

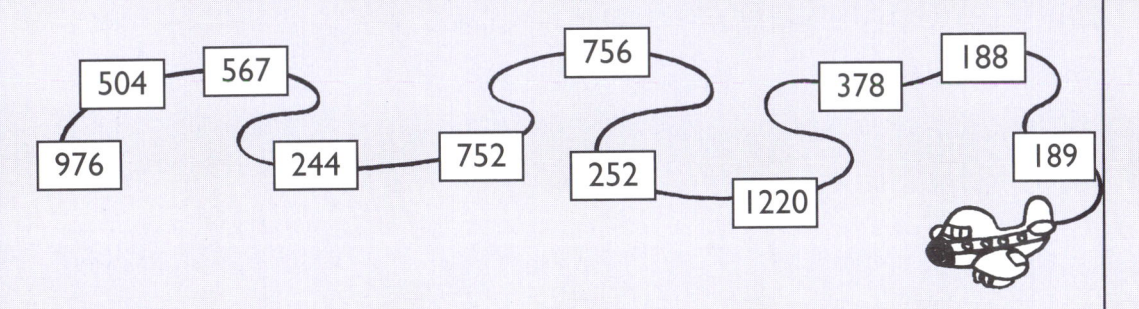

Numbers on the plane: 504, 567, 756, 378, 188, 976, 244, 752, 252, 1220, 189

Use two numbers from the plane to make a fraction equivalent to:

1. $\dfrac{1}{2}$
2. $\dfrac{1}{3}$
3. $\dfrac{3}{4}$
4. $\dfrac{1}{4}$
5. $\dfrac{1}{5}$
6. $\dfrac{3}{8}$
7. $\dfrac{4}{5}$
8. $\dfrac{2}{3}$

Can you find more than one equivalent for any of the fractions?

Cards: 0, 1, 2, 3, 4, 5, 6, 7, 8, 9

Use three cards from this set to make as many different proper fractions as you can.

Write the fractions in order.

Example

Cards: 2, 4, 5

$\dfrac{2}{54}, \dfrac{2}{45}, \dfrac{4}{52}, \dfrac{5}{42}, \dfrac{4}{25}, \dfrac{5}{24}$

Repeat with three more cards.

Draw a 0 to 1 number line and write labels for each of your fractions.

Walk graph

Roshan walks 20 km. He draws a line graph of the walk.

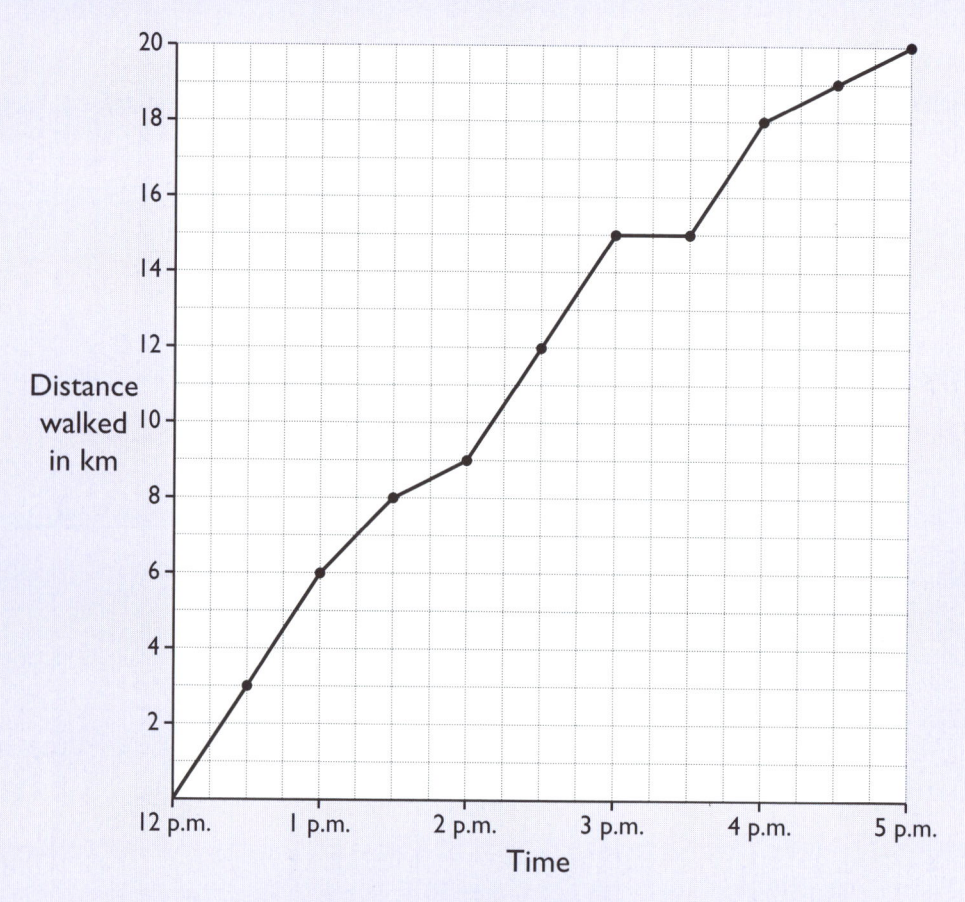

Line Graph to show Roshan's progress

1. How far does Roshan walk between 4 p.m. and 5 p.m.?

2. How far does Roshan walk between 2:30 p.m. and 3:15 p.m.?

3. Roshan stops for a break. At what time does he stop?

4. How many kilometres does he walk per hour on average?

5. What is his average speed between 1 p.m. and 2 p.m.?

6. During which time periods does he walk at 6 km per hour?

Make up a journey and draw a line graph to show progress.

Mean, median and range

Write the mean, the median and the range of each set of data. Use a calculator to help you.

1. 18 000   38 000   21 000   74 000
            37 000   8000
   56 000   16 000   2000

2. 17 000   15 018   20 900   9089
            10 000   17 000
   7000   30 900   11 000

3. 7572   9000   7500   5000
          3000   7500   5000
   4000   4000   8003   4360

4. 3330   3100   4690   6200
                 5800   3312
          4400   3400   2200

5. 1246   9243   5662   8796
          9874   4119   4830
   4230   7657   8791   4445

6. 3753   5843   8939   96 156
          70 289 93 137 9503
   1198   1985   7201   16 101

Find the mean, median and range of three sets put together.

9

Conversion graph

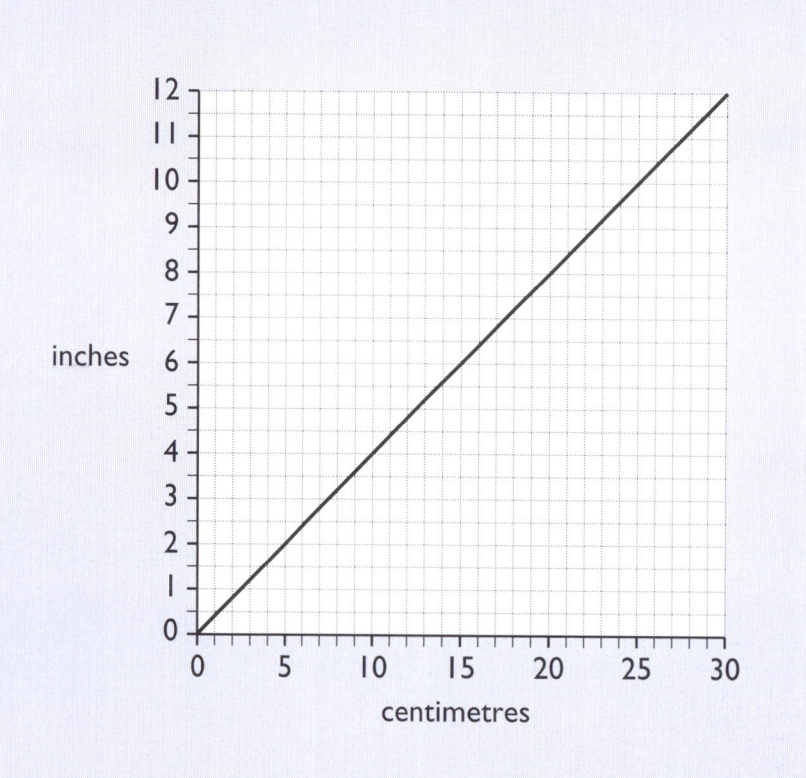

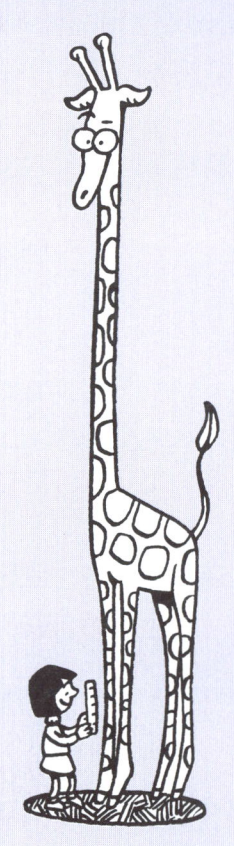

Use the conversion graph to convert each length to the nearest half an inch.

1. 15 cm
2. 5 cm
3. 17 cm
4. 26 cm
5. 19 cm
6. 22 cm
7. 7 cm
8. 27 cm
9. 9 cm
10. 29 cm
11. 17 cm
12. 24 cm

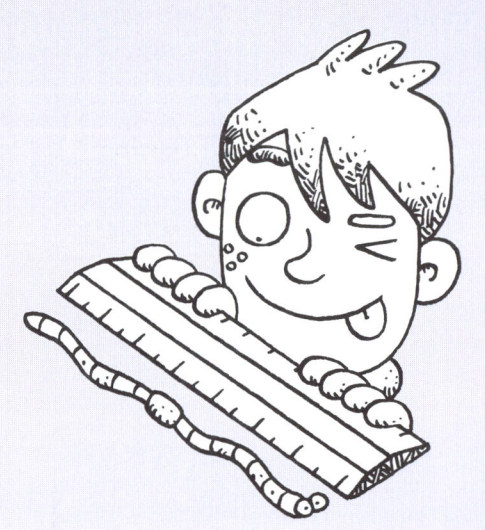

Angles

Calculate the size of each missing angle.

1.

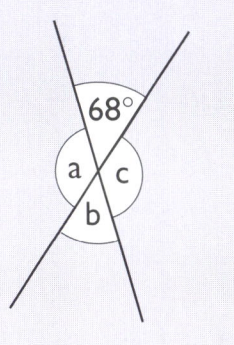

2.

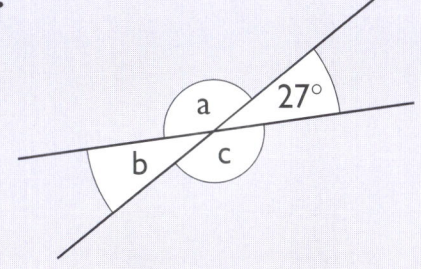

3.

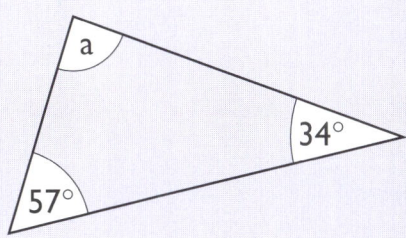

4.

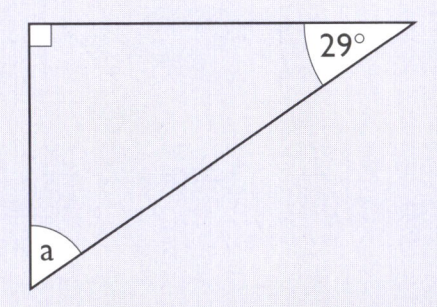

5.

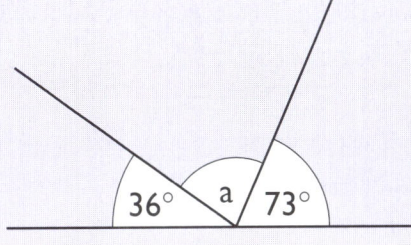

6.

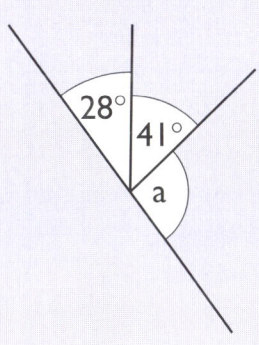

7.

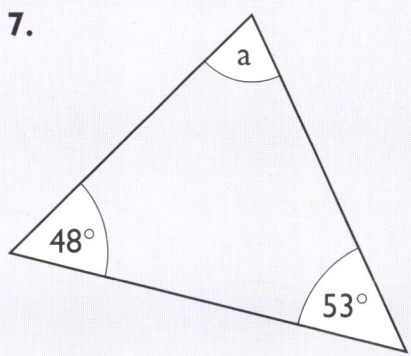

8.

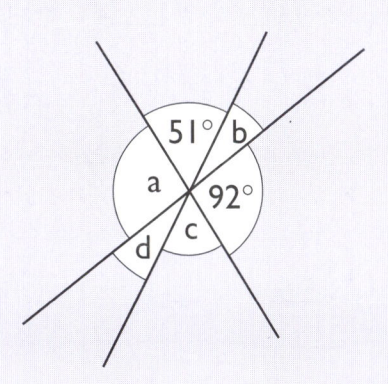

Recipe book

Write out each list of ingredients for 3 people.

Spicy beans – serves 2

- 20 ml olive oil
- 1 onion
- ½ teaspoon chilli powder
- 150 g baked beans

Winter vegetable soup – serves 4

- 20 g butter
- 1 tbsp oil
- 200 g onion
- 200 g leek
- 200 g carrot
- 60 g celery
- 180 g potato
- 120 g swede
- 1 litre milk

Write out each list of ingredients in grams. Remember, 1 oz is about 25 g.

Flapjacks

- 4 oz unsalted butter
- 2 oz caster sugar
- 4 oz golden syrup
- 8 oz rolled oats
- 2 tsp ground ginger

Carrot cake

- 5 oz carrots
- 3 oz grated apple
- 3 oz sultanas
- 7 oz self-raising flour
- 6 oz caster sugar
- 1 teaspoon baking powder
- 3 eggs
- 4 tablespoons vegetable oil
- ½ teaspoon vanilla
- ½ teaspoon cinnamon powder
- 4 oz cream cheese
- 5 oz butter
- 9 oz icing sugar

Find a recipe in grams and convert the weights into ounces.

Space travel

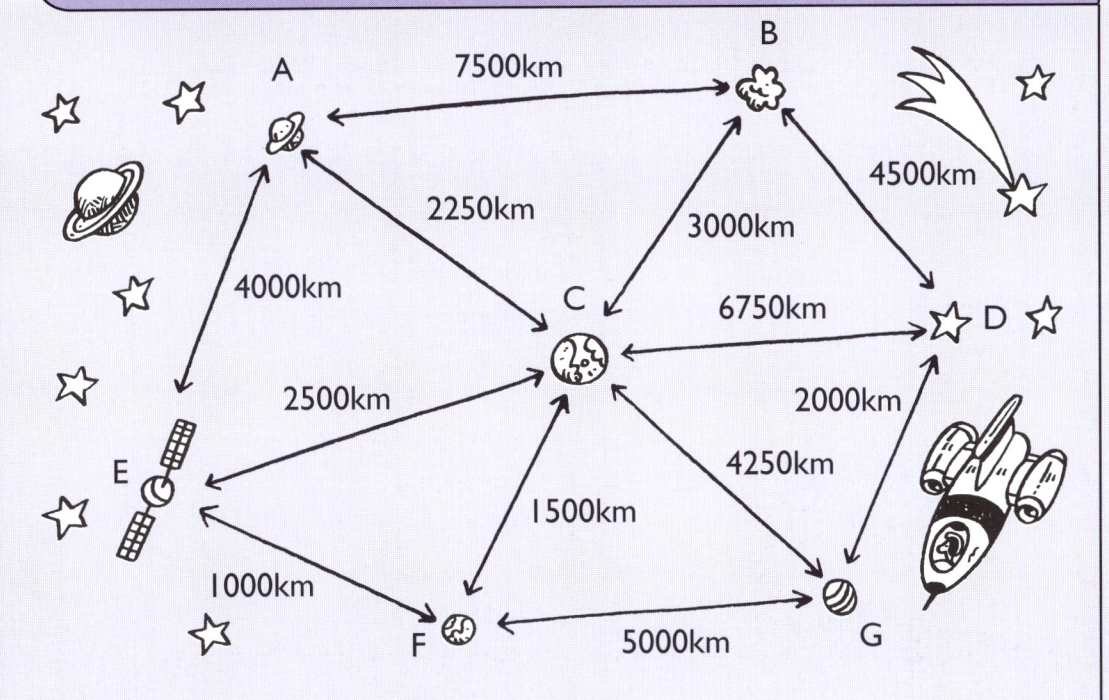

The spaceship travels at 3000 km an hour.

Write how long it takes to travel from:

1. A to B
2. E to F
3. G to F to E
4. B to C to F
5. C to D to B
6. C to E to F
7. F to G to C
8. E to C to A

The flying saucer travels at 10000 km per hour.

Write how long it takes to travel from:

9. B to C
10. A to B
11. F to C to E
12. F to G to D
13. A to B to C
14. A to E to C
15. B to C to E
16. G to C to D

Map

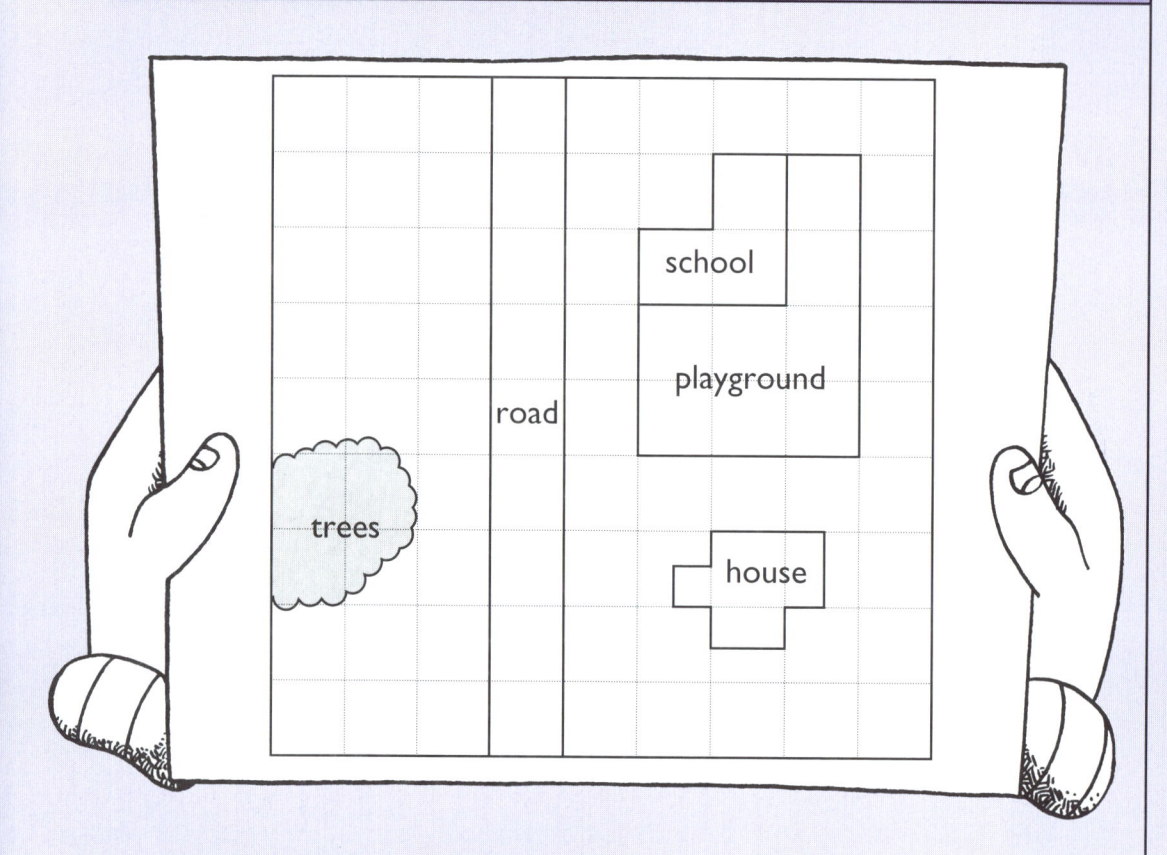

The scale of the map is 1:1200.

So 1 cm on the map represents 1200 cm on the ground.

Write:

1. the length of the road

2. the area of the school

3. the area of the playground

4. the area of the house

5. the area covered by the whole map

6. the approximate area of the trees.

Jackpot

Each prize is shared between 10 people. Write how much each person gets.

1. £796 000
2. £33 650
3. £64 061

4. £45 378
5. £108 725
6. £37 419

7. £28 402
8. £63 888
9. £71 624

10. £1 536 000
11. £26 305
12. £181 953

13. If each person then shared their prize with 9 other people, how much would each person get?

In another competition, 100 people share the prize. Write the total prize money if each person receives:

14. £8864·20
15. £9086·85
16. £1814·50

17. £333·33
18. £197·65
19. £2270·23

Write how many people share a prize if:

20. the total prize money is £12678 and they each receive £126·78

21. the total prize money is £23760 and they each receive £23·76

22. the total prize money is £907800 and they each receive £90780

23. the total prize money is £1146 and they each receive £114·60.

Housemates

James, Leo and Ayesha share a house. These are their bills:

Water £27.30 every 3 months

Gas £15.60 every month

Electricity £31.50 every 2 months

Telephone £41.22 every 2 months

TV licence £104 every year

Food £59.40 every 2 weeks

Newspapers £5.70 every week

They work out how much they have each spent on the telephone and share the rest of the bills fairly.

1. How much do they each spend on food in one week?
2. The cost of a TV licence goes up 10%. What is the new price?
3. James gets a Sunday newspaper which costs 70p a week. How much would the house save on newsapers in a year if he changed to a newspaper costing 55p?
4. How much do the housemates spend altogether on gas, water and electricity in 6 months?
5. How much do the housemates spend on the telephone in a year?
6. The next gas bill is 15% higher. James, Leo and Ayesha each pay $\frac{1}{3}$ of the bill. How much do they each pay?
7. The housemates work out how much of the telephone bill they must pay. Ayesha must pay $\frac{1}{6}$, James must pay $\frac{1}{3}$ and Leo must pay $\frac{1}{2}$. How much do they each pay? How much do they each spend on the telephone in a year?
8. Leo moves out of the house on 20th June. What fraction of that month's gas bill must he pay? Draw a grid to help you find the answer.
9. James and Ayesha share the cost of the gas for the rest of the month. How much do they each have to pay in total for gas in June?

Work out how much the housemates spend on bills in a year.

Factors

Find the highest common factor for each set of cards.

1. 208, 264, 248, 296, 200

2. 220, 198, 176, 264, 242

3. 231, 220, 253, 209, 275

4. 258, 294, 192, 240, 282

5. 189, 252, 210, 126, 105

6. 210, 280, 294, 238, 266

With a friend, each write a 3-digit number. What is the highest common factor?

Prime addition

Write out all the prime numbers between 1 and 100. Remember, a prime number only has 2 factors: itself and 1. Use your list to help you with the questions.

Write 2 prime numbers which add to make:

1. 32
2. 26
3. 45
4. 30
5. 68
6. 24
7. 56
8. 78

Find:

9. 4 different pairs of prime numbers which add to make 80.

10. 6 different pairs of prime numbers which add to make 100.

11. 3 prime numbers which total 35.

12. 3 prime numbers which total 65.

13. 4 prime numbers which total 90.

14. 4 prime numbers which total 100.

Roll a dice twice to make a 2-digit number. How many ways of making it by adding prime numbers can you find?

Card addition

Sort the number cards to make two 4-digit numbers and a 3-digit number which add to make each total.

You must use each card once for each total.

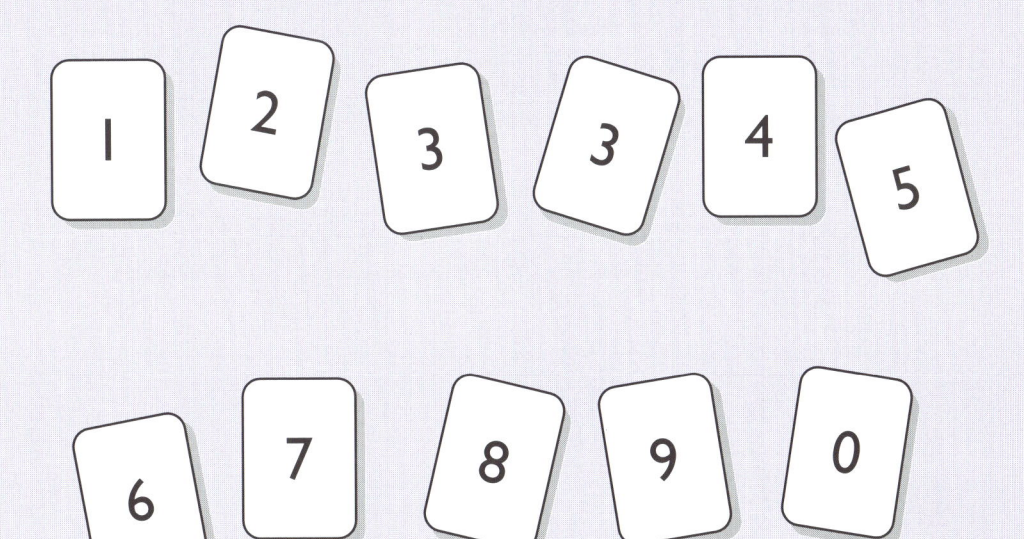

Example 3321 + 6789 + 450 = 10560

1. 8517
2. 9471
3. 18 003
4. 14 781
5. 6690
6. 8355
7. 16 068
8. 14 916

9. What is the smallest total you can make this way?

10. What is the largest?

Make ten more totals this way. List them in ascending order.

Superbrain

In the Superbrain quiz contestants must answer 20 questions.
They are given 2 points for a right answer, and ⁻3 points for a wrong answer.
Write each person's score.

1. 13 right / 7 wrong
2. 11 right / 9 wrong
3. 2 right / 18 wrong
4. 10 right / 10 wrong
5. 8 right / 12 wrong
6. 6 right / 14 wrong
7. 3 right / 17 wrong
8. 9 right / 11 wrong

How many right and wrong answers has each person given so far?

9. 9 questions / ⁻17 points
10. 17 questions / ⁻16 points
11. 13 questions / 1 point
12. 18 questions / ⁻9 points
13. 11 questions / 12 points
14. 14 questions / ⁻27 points
15. 16 questions / 7 points
16. 15 questions / 15 points

What would each person's score be in questions 1 to 8 if they were given 5 points for a right answer and ⁻7 for a wrong answer?

Rockets

Write out the multiplications or divisions for each rocket.

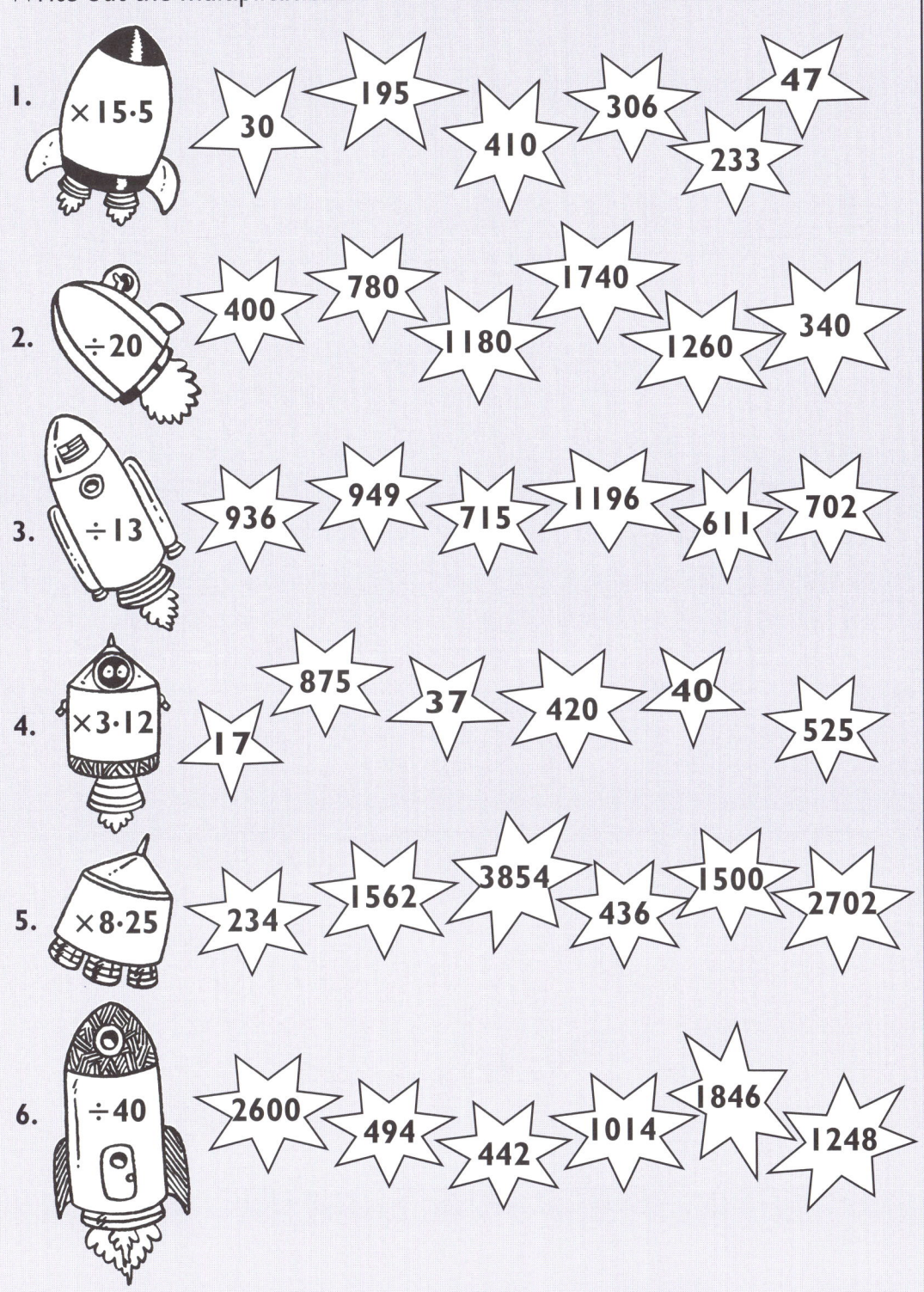

1. ×15·5 — 30, 195, 410, 306, 233, 47

2. ÷20 — 400, 780, 1180, 1740, 1260, 340

3. ÷13 — 936, 949, 715, 1196, 611, 702

4. ×3·12 — 17, 875, 37, 420, 40, 525

5. ×8·25 — 234, 1562, 3854, 436, 1500, 2702

6. ÷40 — 2600, 494, 442, 1014, 1846, 1248

Problems

Find 3 consecutive numbers which add to make:

1. 81
2. 57
3. 339
4. 504
5. 486
6. 645

7. Mr Mint works in a building which is 35 storeys high. On each of the first 13 storeys there are 134 windows. On each of the next 18 storeys there are 126 windows. On each of the other floors there are 106 windows.

   How many windows altogether?

8. There are 500 seats in the cinema. Adult tickets cost £4·75, child tickets cost £2·80.

   On Monday 220 adults went to the cinema. In total, the cinema took £1465·00.

   How many children were there? How many empty seats were there?

9. On Saturday the cinema was full. £1282·50 worth of adult tickets were sold.

   How much was spent on child tickets?

Gardens

Write the area of lawn in each garden.

1.

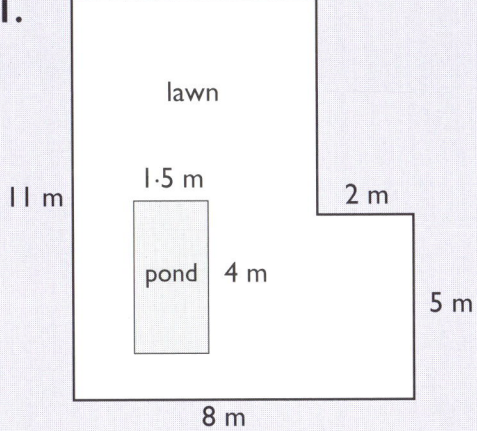

lawn
11 m
1.5 m
2 m
pond 4 m
5 m
8 m

2.

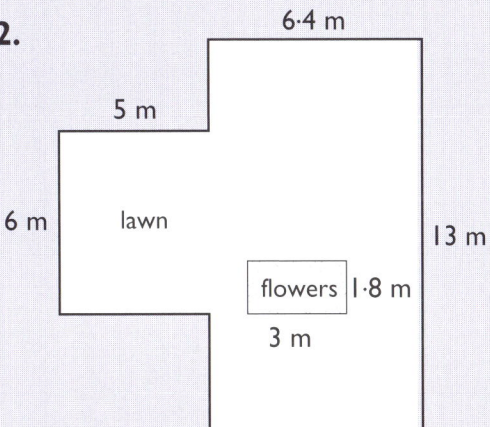

6.4 m
5 m
6 m lawn
13 m
flowers 1.8 m
3 m

3.

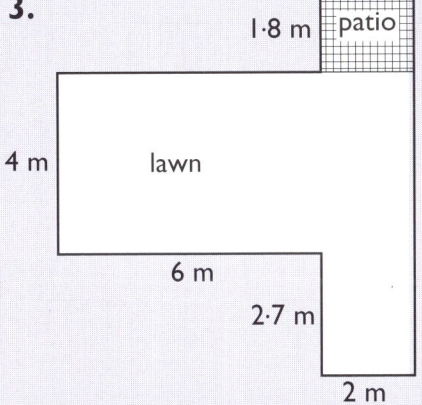

1.8 m patio
4 m
lawn
6 m
2.7 m
2 m

4.

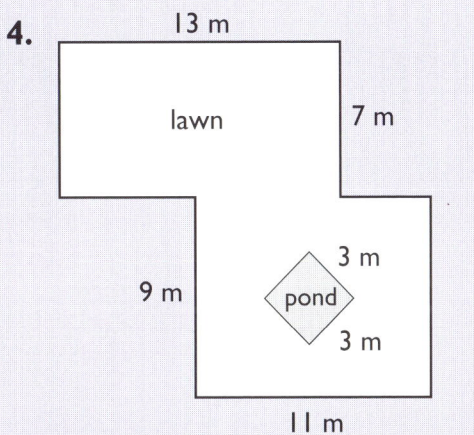

13 m
lawn
7 m
9 m
3 m
pond
3 m
11 m

5.

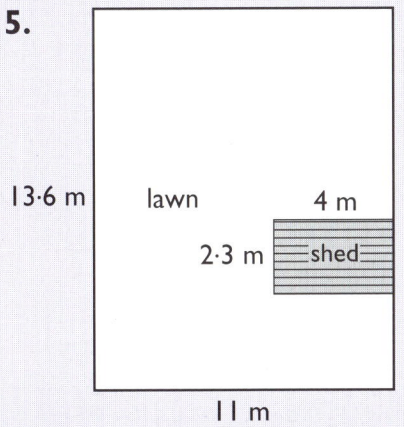

13.6 m
lawn
4 m
2.3 m shed
11 m

6.

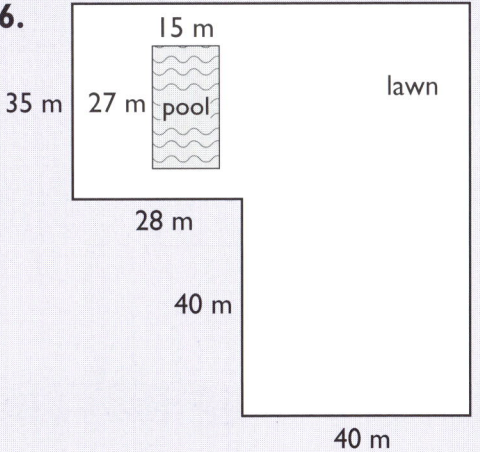

15 m
lawn
35 m 27 m pool
28 m
40 m
40 m

23

Pascal's triangle

This is a famous pattern known as Pascal's Triangle. Can you work out how the triangle works?

```
                        1
                     1     1
                  1     2     1
               1     3     3     1
            1     4     6     4     1
         1     5    10    10     5     1
      1     6    15    20    15     6     1
   1     7    21    35    35    21     7     1
1     8    28    56    70    56    28     8     1
```

Copy the triangle and write the next 2 rows.

Find the mystery numbers.

1. It is the largest number in a row which adds up to 64.

2. The eight numbers surrounding this number add up to 42.

3. The eight numbers surrounding this number add up to 157.

4. This number is a multiple of 3. It appears in a row which adds up to 128.

Write the next 3 rows of the triangle.

Waiter worries

Walter the waiter has lost his price list. He needs to add up a customer's bill, but the only way he can work out the price of each item is by looking at old bills. He knows everything costs an exact number of pounds.

Can you work out the price of each item and the total bill?

5 lemonades
2 salads
3 pasta
2 ice creams
Total ?

1 pasta
1 lemonade
2 salads
Total £10

3 ice creams
4 lemonades
1 pasta
Total £21

3 salads
4 pasta
Total £26

2 salads
3 pasta
1 lemonade
Total £20

Fraction grid

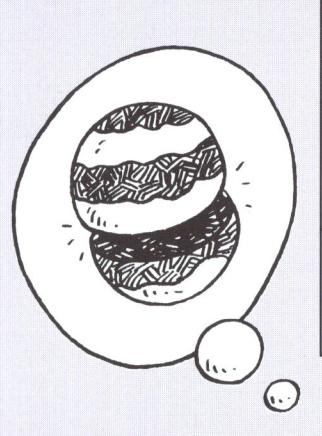

4	7	9	2
24	8	3	10
6	21	12	14

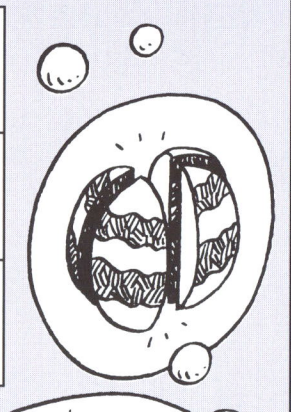

Use the numbers on the grid to make:

1. 5 fractions equivalent to $\frac{1}{3}$

2. 4 fractions equivalent to $\frac{2}{3}$

3. 2 fractions equivalent to $\frac{1}{6}$

4. a fraction equivalent to $\frac{5}{6}$

5. 2 fractions equivalent to $\frac{3}{7}$

6. 2 fractions equivalent to $\frac{4}{7}$

7. 2 improper fractions equivalent to 7

8. 5 improper fractions equivalent to 3.

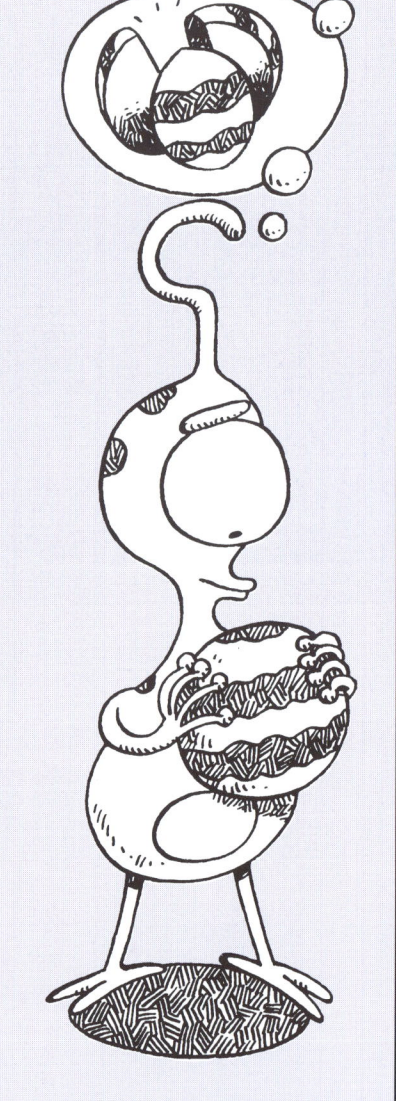

Can you make 10 pairs of fractions which add to make 1?
Do not use a grid number more than once in the same pair.

Fractions

Write:

1. $\frac{4}{9}$ of 63   270   180   54   81

2. $\frac{7}{8}$ of 72   80   56   32   48

3. $\frac{8}{10}$ of 270   400   1500   1000   100

4. $\frac{3}{5}$ of 225   1500   800   300   445

5. $\frac{11}{12}$ of 600   804   48 000   3600   240

6. $\frac{11}{20}$ of 80   1800   620   8200   600

Write:

1. 80% $\frac{1}{5}$ $\frac{8}{16}$ 0·5 $\frac{1}{4}$ of   £7500

2. $\frac{90}{100}$ 50%   0.25   0.75   15%   of   £1000

3. 45%   0.4 $\frac{25}{100}$ 8%   250%   of   £900

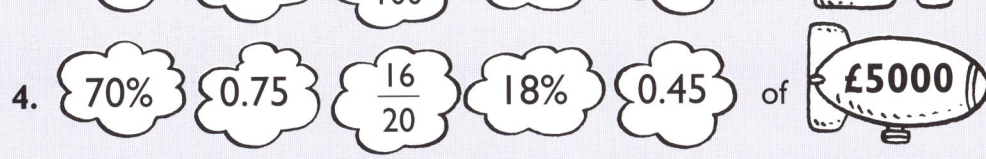

4. 70%   0.75 $\frac{16}{20}$ 18%   0.45   of   £5000

Triangles

Describe the properties of and draw:

1. an equilateral triangle
2. an isosceles triangle
3. a scalene triangle
4. a right-angled triangle.

Measure each angle in each triangle and label them.

Use a protractor to draw triangles with the two angles given.

5. 33°, 57°
6. 120°, 28°
7. 98°, 69°
8. 36°, 84°
9. 60°, 110°
10. 80°, 47°
11. 53°, 68°
12. 71°, 69°

Calculate the size of the third angle and then check your triangles with a protractor.

Are they accurate?

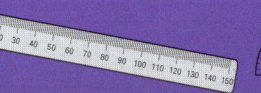

Calculate the area of three of your triangles.

Problems

1. Hans runs round a 400 m track 15 times. How many kilometres has he run?

2. 68 cm is cut from a 17 m rope, and the rest of it is cut into 32 equal pieces. How long is each piece?

3. A roll of ribbon is cut into 47 pieces. Each piece is 3·7 cm long. How long was the roll of ribbon?

4. Lemonade cans hold 330 mℓ each. There are 12 cans in a pack. How many litres of lemonade in three packs?

5. A bottle of vanilla essence holds 0·125 ℓ. How many 5 mℓ teaspoons can be poured from the bottle?

6. A piece of wood is 27·68 m long. 5 pieces of equal length are cut off, and a piece measuring 3·68 m is left. How long is each of the 5 pieces?

7. Kerry has a bucket which holds 3·8 litres and a jug which holds 0·4 litres. How many jugfuls of water does she need to fill the bucket?

8. A bus travels 15·8 km in one journey. It makes the journey 6 times a day on weekdays and 4 times a day on Saturdays and Sundays. How far does the bus travel in a week?

9. Simon travels 54·6 km by car and then rides 1350 m on his bike. How many kilometres has he travelled? How many metres?

10. Ali cycles to school every weekday, to his friend's house every Saturday and to football practice every Sunday. Ali's school is 1·325 km from home, his friend lives 943 m from his house and the football field is 2016 m away. How far does he cycle in a week?

Space stations

Distance between space stations

Distance in km	Zax	Tropple	Nilda	Chorm	Dring
Dring	13130 km	26550 km	19800 km	15500 km	–
Chorm	23115 km	16225 km	23130 km	–	
Nilda	20145 km	18675 km	–		
Tropple	19240 km	–			
Zax	–				

How fast is each alien's spaceship? Write your answers in kilometres per minute.

1. A travels from Nilda to Chorm in $1\frac{1}{2}$ hours.

2. B travels from Dring to Tropple in $2\frac{1}{2}$ hours.

3. C travels from Nilda to Dring in 50 minutes.

4. D travels from Zax to Dring in 2 hours 10 minutes.

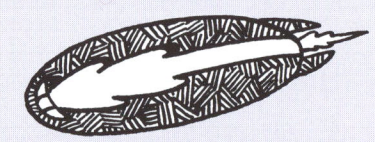

5. E travels from Zax to to Chorm in 5 hours 45 minutes.

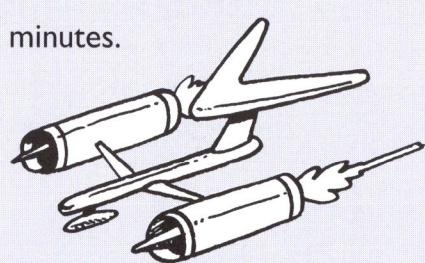

6. F travels from Zax to Tropple in 4 hours 20 minutes.

Calculate each journey time for a space ship which travels at 5 km/minute.

Building a den

Karim and Shula are building a den. They have £300 to spend.

They already have enough materials to make the roof.
Wall sections are a metre long and cost £4 each.
Square floor tiles measuring 1m² cost £8 each.
They must leave a 1m gap in the wall for a door.

What shape den could they build?
Try to find the den with the largest possible area of floor.

Remember not to spend more than £300. How much money will they have left?

Example

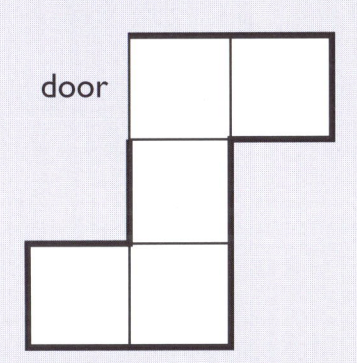

Floor   5 × £8 = £40
Walls   11 × £4 = £44
Total cost £40 + £44 = £84
£300 − £84 = £216
£216 left

What dens could they build for £500?

Brain teasers

Four explorers need to cross a river at night.
The only way across is an old rope bridge. It is only strong enough to hold two people at a time.
It is too dangerous to cross the bridge without a torch. The torch battery will only last 17 minutes.

They all travel at different speeds:
Alf can run across the bridge in **1 minute**.
Basia can skip across the bridge in **2 minutes**.
Chantelle can walk across the bridge in **5 minutes**.
Des can creep across the bridge in **10 minutes**.

Find a way for all the explorers to get across in 17 minutes, always using the torch.
Remember, only two people can be on the bridge at a time!

After they have crossed the bridge, the explorers want to cook some noodles for dinner.

They need to cook the noodles for 9 minutes exactly. They have no clocks or watches – only two sand timers. One lasts 7 minutes. The other lasts 4 minutes.

How can they use the timers to time the noodles for exactly 9 minutes?

Make up a similar puzzle for a friend.

Probability

There are 300 houses in Acacia Avenue. Each house has a painted front door.

88 are red
50 are blue
57 are green
45 are yellow
42 are brown
12 are purple
4 are pink
1 is gold
1 is silver

The probability that a door chosen at random is red is $\frac{88}{300}$.

So the probability that the door is not red is $1 - \frac{88}{300} = 1 - \frac{22}{75} = \frac{53}{75}$

Write the probability that the door is:

1. blue
2. green
3. yellow
4. pink
5. brown
6. silver or gold
7. pink or purple
8. yellow, brown or red
9. gold, green or blue
10. neither blue nor green
11. neither pink nor silver
12. neither purple, nor silver, nor yellow.

Birthday puzzle

Find the age of the other member or members of each family.

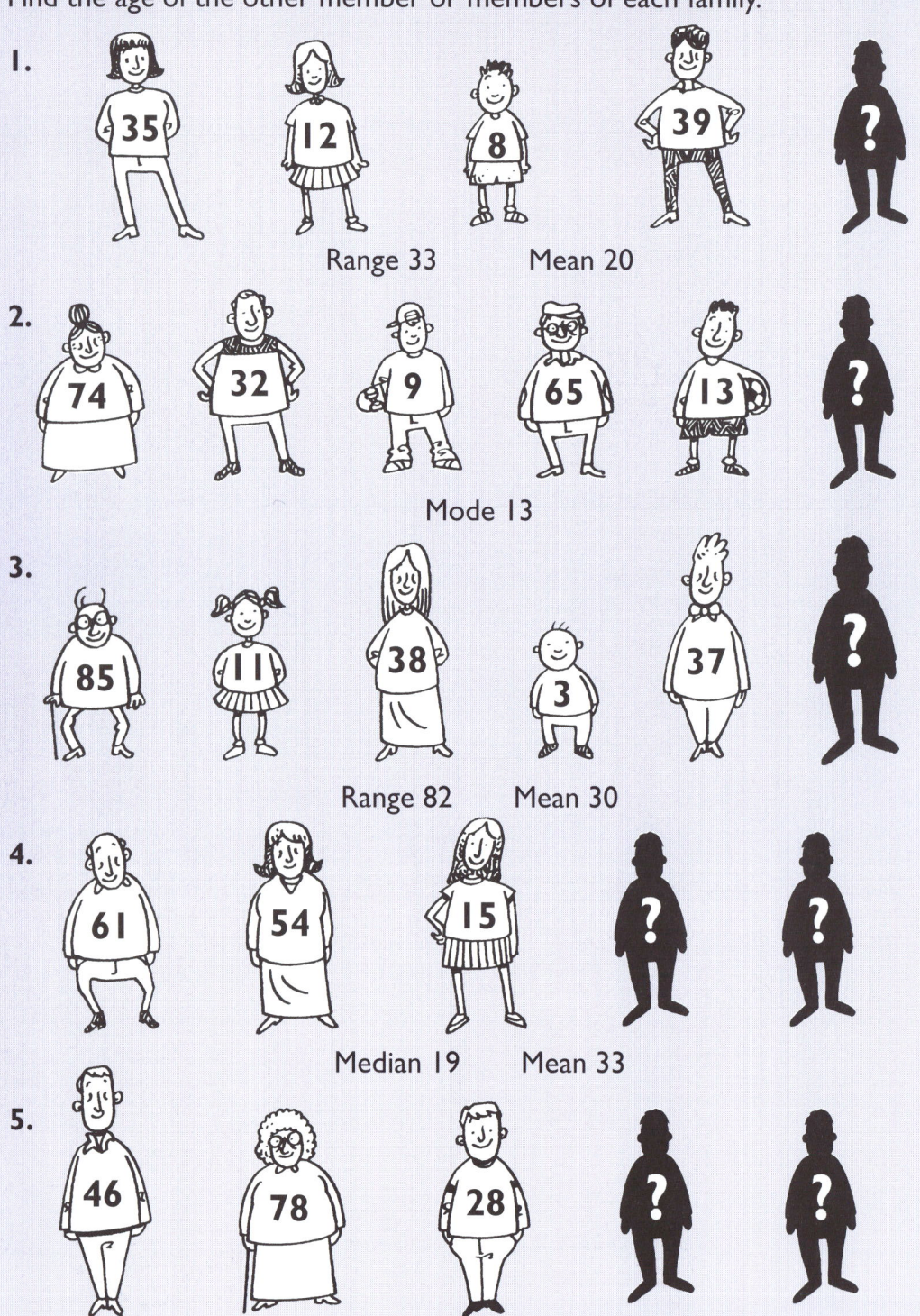

1. 35, 12, 8, 39, ?
   Range 33   Mean 20

2. 74, 32, 9, 65, 13, ?
   Mode 13

3. 85, 11, 38, 3, 37, ?
   Range 82   Mean 30

4. 61, 54, 15, ?, ?
   Median 19   Mean 33

5. 46, 78, 28, ?, ?
   Mean 46   Median 46   Range 51

Can you make up a similar puzzle?

School survey

A survey was carried out to find out how far pupils travel to get to two schools. The results are displayed in two pie charts.

Distance travelled by pupils to Tibblesdale School

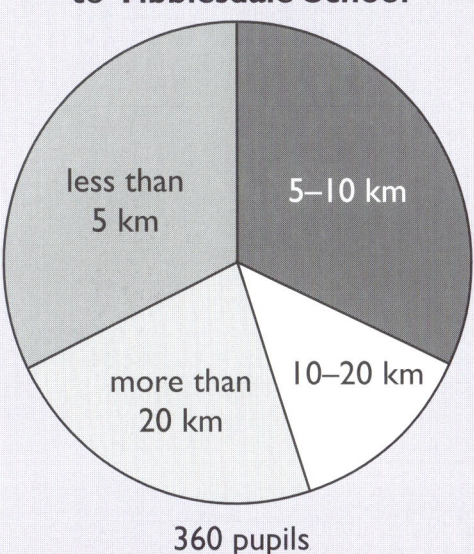

360 pupils

Distance travelled by pupils to Greenridge School

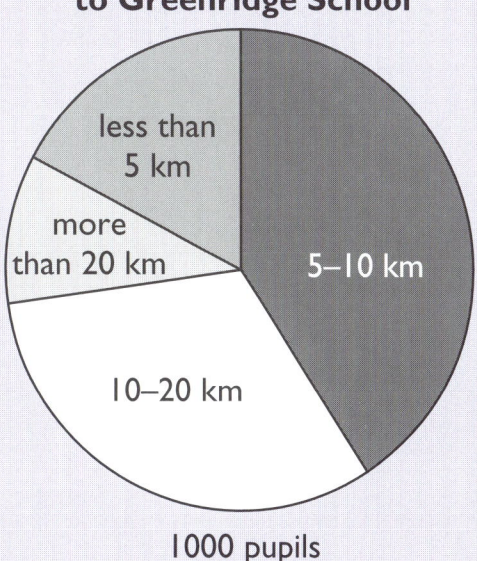

1000 pupils

Write true or false for each statement.

1. About 100 children travel 5–10 km to Tibblesdale.
2. Less than 500 children travel 5–10 km to Greenridge.
3. More than 250 children travel less than 5 km to Greenridge.
4. More than 90 children travel more than 20 km to Tibblesdale.
5. Less than 100 children travel 10–20 km to Tibblesdale.
6. More children travel 10–20 km to Greenridge than to Tibblesdale.
7. More children travel less than 5 km to Tibblesdale than to Greenridge.
8. More children travel more than 20 km to Greenridge than to Tibblesdale.

Write 5 more statements. Swap with a friend. Can you say if they are true or false?

Labyrinth

Each door can only be opened by a key whose number is a factor of the door number. Where will each key allow you to go in the castle?

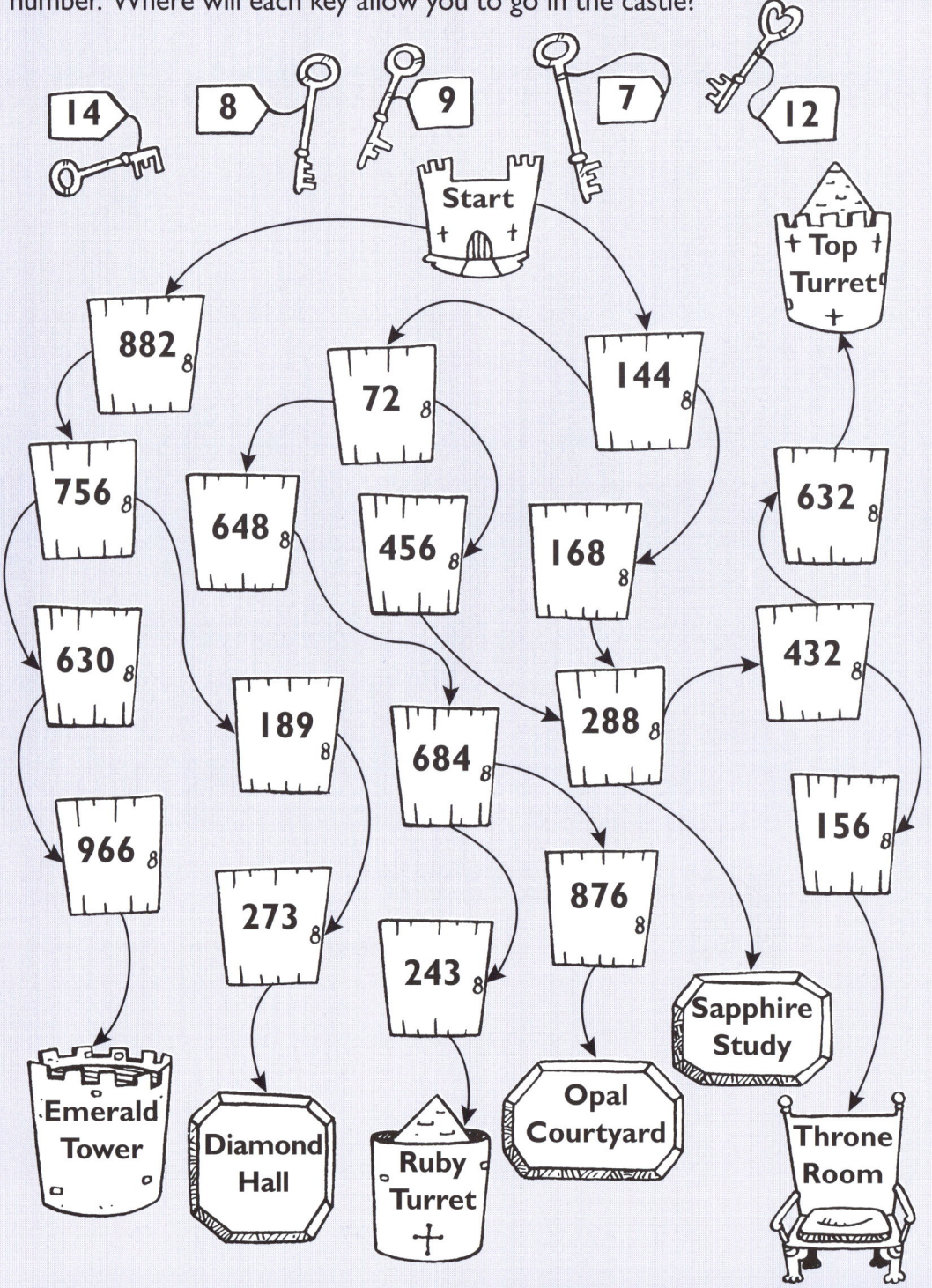

Keys: 14, 8, 9, 7, 12

Doors: 882, 72, 144, 756, 648, 456, 168, 632, 630, 189, 288, 432, 966, 273, 684, 876, 156, 243

Rooms: Emerald Tower, Diamond Hall, Ruby Turret, Opal Courtyard, Sapphire Study, Throne Room, Top Turret

36 — Where would a key with the number 6 allow you to go?

Number clouds

Choose the correct cloud to complete each number sentence.

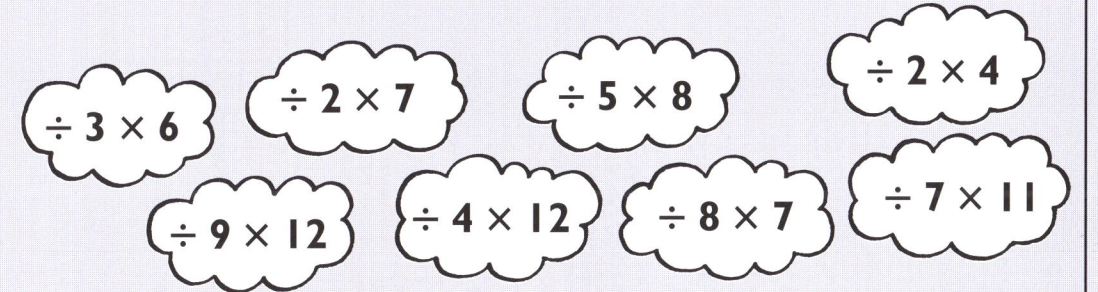

Clouds: ÷ 3 × 6, ÷ 2 × 7, ÷ 5 × 8, ÷ 2 × 4, ÷ 9 × 12, ÷ 4 × 12, ÷ 8 × 7, ÷ 7 × 11

1. 26 ◯ = 52
2. 81 ◯ = 108
3. 48 ◯ = 42
4. 32 ◯ = 112
5. 80 ◯ = 128
6. 63 ◯ = 99
7. 48 ◯ = 144
8. 39 ◯ = 78

Divide a number from the circle by a number from the triangle to make each total.

Circle: 3068, 225, 2781, 744, 1944, 588, 696, 1420, 869, 3861, 936, 423, 1056, 702

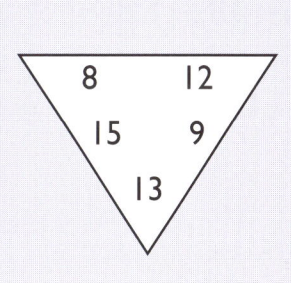

Triangle: 8, 12, 15, 9, 13

1. 15
2. 87
3. 309
4. 162
5. 243
6. 78
7. 54
8. 88
9. 47
10. 49
11. 297
12. 62

Phone bill

Call type	Length in minutes and seconds	Cost
UK	11 m 5 s	£1·33
International	14 m 50 s	£3·56
UK	9 m 10 s	£1·10
International	7 m 40 s	£1·84
UK	12 m 45 s	£1·53
UK	32 m 15 s	£3·87
UK	38 m 40 s	£4·64
UK	19 m 40 s	£2·36
International	17 m 5 s	£4·10
UK	8 m 55 s	£1·07
UK	13 m	£1·56
International	47 m	£11·28
UK	0 m 40 s	£0·08
UK	5 m 25 s	£0·65
UK	50 m 5 s	£6·01
International	16 m 30 s	£3·96
UK	11 m 20 s	£1·36
International	6 m 25 s	£1·54

1. What is the charge for every 5 seconds of a UK call?
2. What is the charge for every 5 seconds of an international call?
3. What is the range of call costs?
4. What is the range of international call costs?
5. What is the range of UK call costs?
6. What is the mean call cost?
7. What is the mean UK call cost?
8. What is the mean international call cost?
9. What is the range of the call lengths?
10. What is the range of international call lengths?
11. What is the range of UK call lengths?
12. What is the median call length?
13. What is the median length of UK calls?
14. What is the median length of international calls?

Cycle race

Jason and Amy raced each other 50 km on their bikes. They started at 1 p.m. Copy the axes below on squared paper. Use the information in the table to draw a graph for Amy and a graph for Jason.

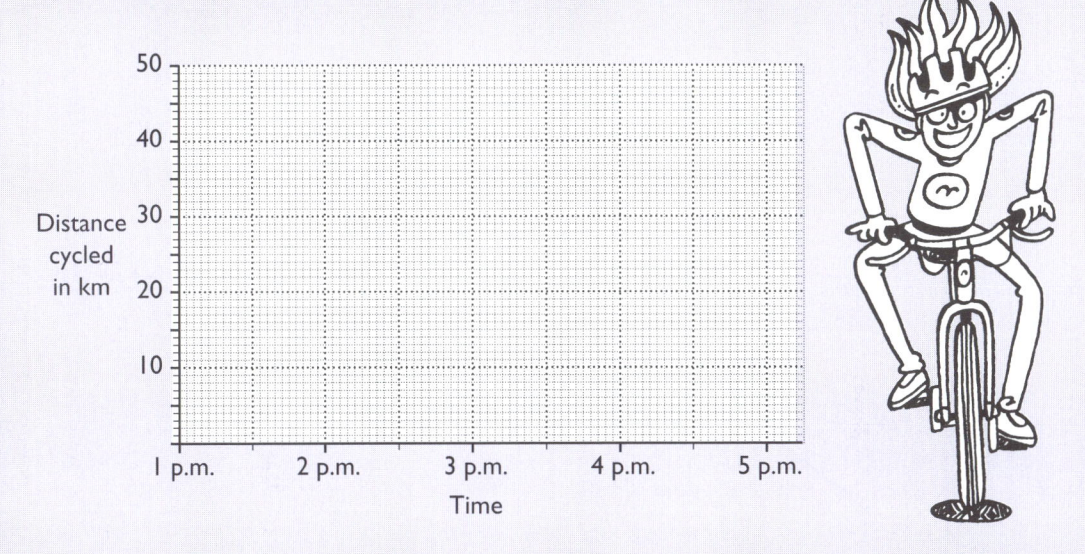

Time	Distance cycled by Amy	Distance cycled by Jason
1:30 p.m.	10 km	10 km
2:00 p.m.	15 km	20 km
2:30 p.m.	20 km	25 km
3:00 p.m.	30 km	28 km
3:30 p.m.	33 km	35 km
4:00 p.m.	40 km	43 km
4:30 p.m.	47 km	50 km
5:00 p.m.	50 km	50 km

What was each cyclist's average speed?

Mystery angles

Calculate the missing angles.

1.

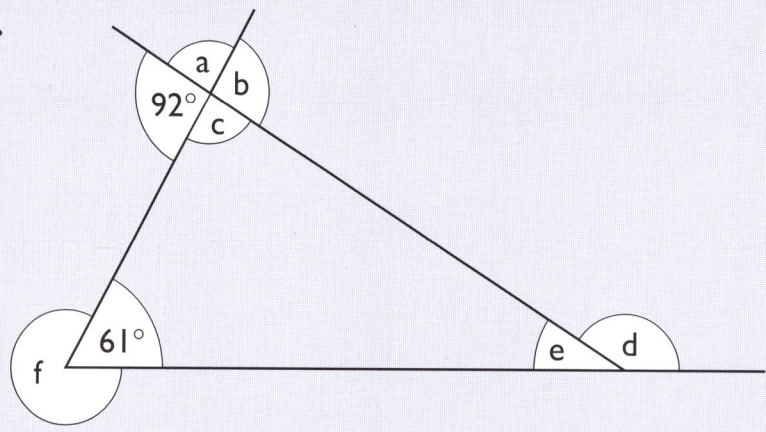

2.

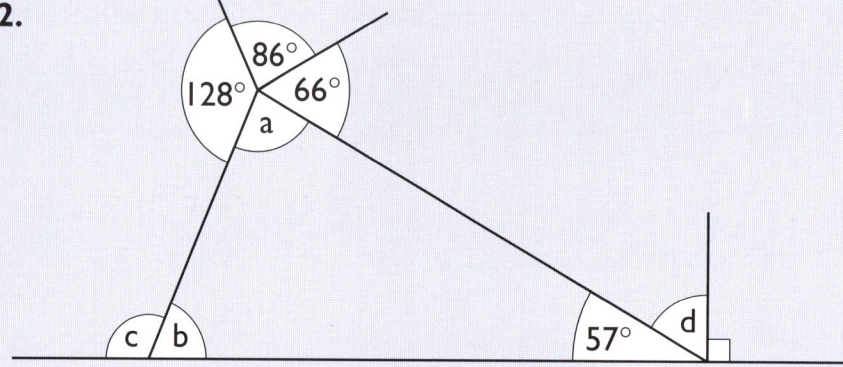

3.

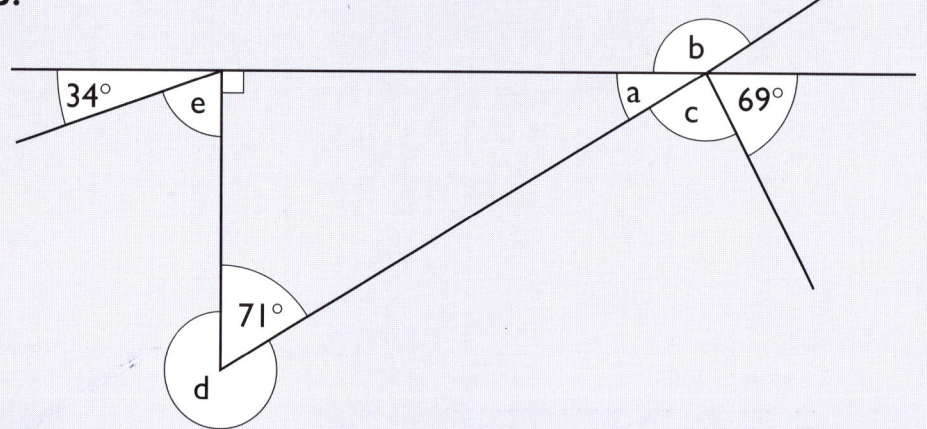

Triangles

The area of a triangle can be worked out using this formula:

area = (base × height) ÷ 2

Example

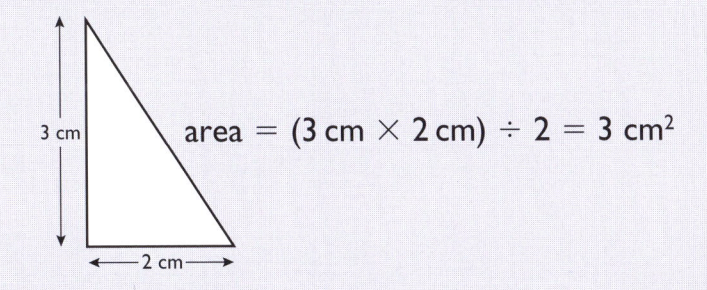

area = (3 cm × 2 cm) ÷ 2 = 3 cm²

Work out the area of each triangle.

1. 5 m, 4 m

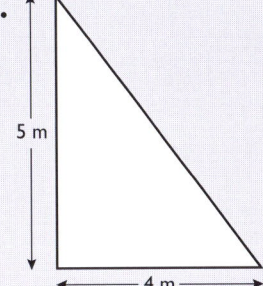

2. 6 cm, 11 cm

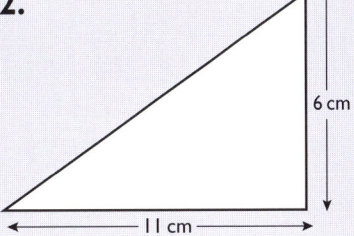

3. 13 cm, 7 cm

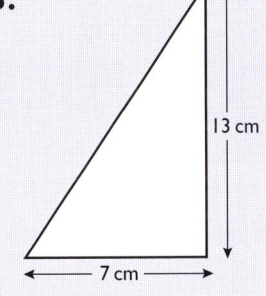

4. 8 m, 9 m

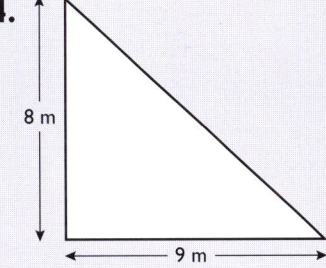

5. 8 cm, 12 cm

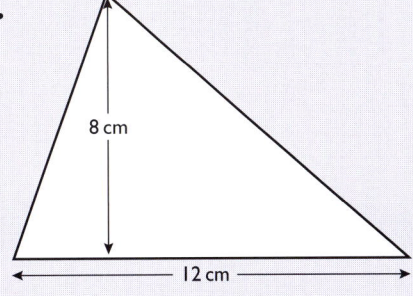

6. 6 m, 15 m

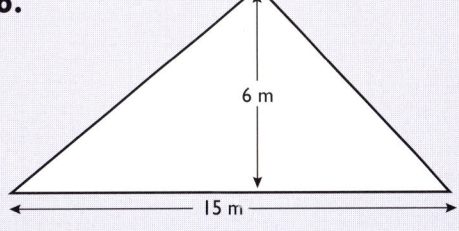

Temperature and weight

Use the formula to convert each temperature from Fahrenheit (°F) to Centigrade (°C).

Round your answers to one decimal place.

temperature in °C = (temperature in °F − 32) × 5 ÷ 9

1. 70°F
2. 65°F
3. 51°F
4. 44°F
5. 32°F
6. 82°F
7. 57°F
8. 28°F
9. 30°F

The Green family weigh 200 kg altogether.

The family are Mum, Dad, Jake and Emily.

Jake and Emily weigh 88 kg together.

Emily weighs 20% more than Jake.

Mum weighs 25% more than Emily.

How much does Dad weigh?

Sports shops

These are the prices at Supersport:

Tennis
Tennis racket	£27·50
Tube of tennis balls	£4·85

Football
Football	£6·60
Pair of football shorts	£12·40
Pair of football socks	£3·20

Basketball
Basketball	£8·50
Basketball net	£37·80

Swimming
Snorkel	£5·80
Pair of swimming trunks	£8·00
Swimming costume	£11·60
Pair of flippers	£3·20

At Sport Stuff tennis equipment costs 20% less than at Supersport, football equipment costs 10% more, swimming equipment costs 5% more and basketball equipment costs the same.

At Mega Sport tennis equipment costs 20% more than at Supersport, football equipment costs 15% less, swimming equipment costs the same and basketball equipment costs 10% less.

Work out where it would be cheapest to buy each shopping list.

1.
   1 tennis racket
   1 pair of football shorts
   1 basketball net
   1 snorkel

2.
   2 tubes tennis balls
   1 pair of football socks
   1 pair of flippers
   1 swimming costume

3.
   1 football
   1 basketball net
   3 basketballs
   1 pair of swimming trunks

4.
   1 tennis racket
   1 football
   1 pair of football shorts
   2 pairs swimming trunks
   2 swimming costumes

5.
   4 tennis rackets
   2 tubes of tennis balls
   3 footballs
   1 snorkel

6.
   1 football
   1 basketball
   2 pairs swimming trunks
   3 pairs flippers
   2 tubes tennis balls

Flower power

Multiply each petal number by the number in the centre of the flower.

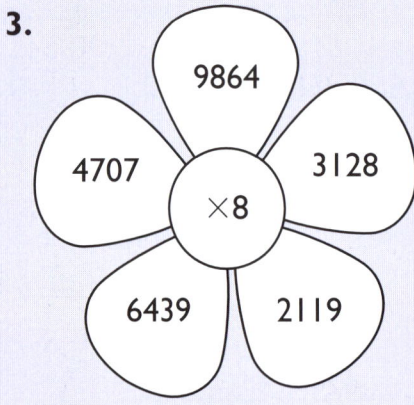

1. Centre: ×2·9; Petals: 2895, 3516, 1798, 9909, 6052

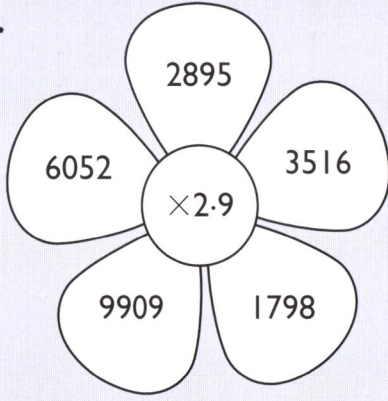

2. Centre: ×4·1; Petals: 19, 37, 73, 58, 64

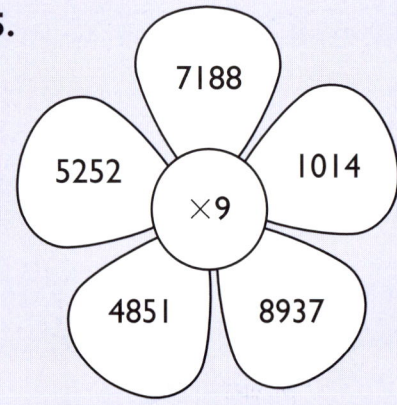

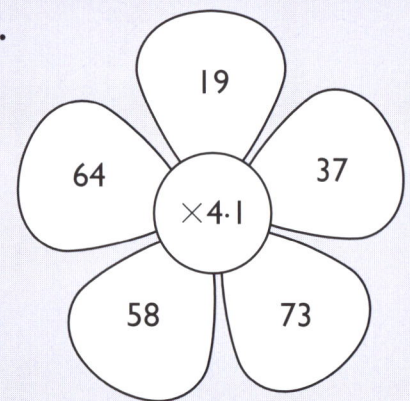

3. Centre: ×8; Petals: 9864, 3128, 2119, 6439, 4707

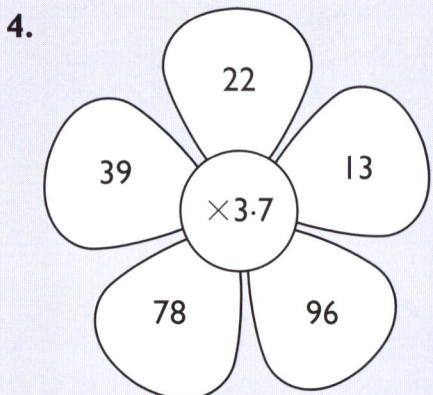

4. Centre: ×3·7; Petals: 22, 13, 96, 78, 39

5. Centre: ×9; Petals: 7188, 1014, 8937, 4851, 5252

6. Centre: ×4·5; Petals: 2·6, 4·8, 7·3, 8·4, 3·9

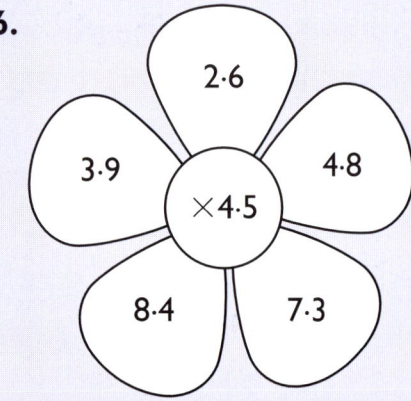

Factors

Write the highest common factor of each set.

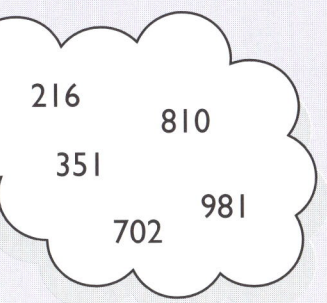

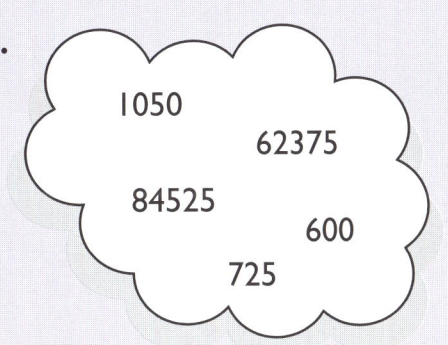

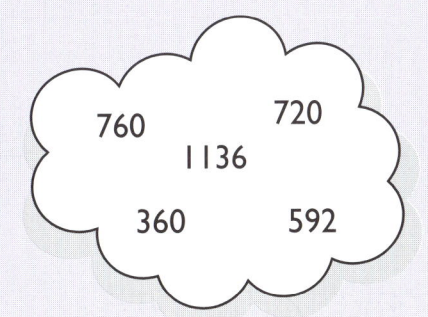

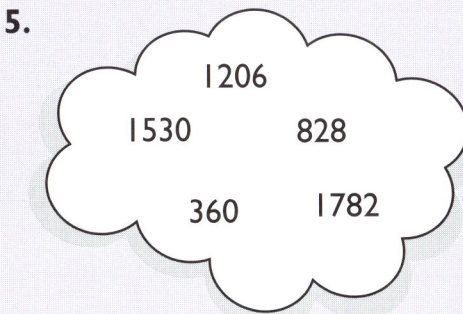

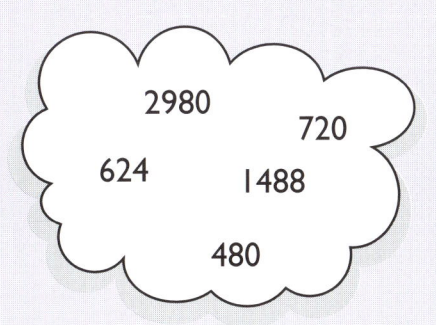

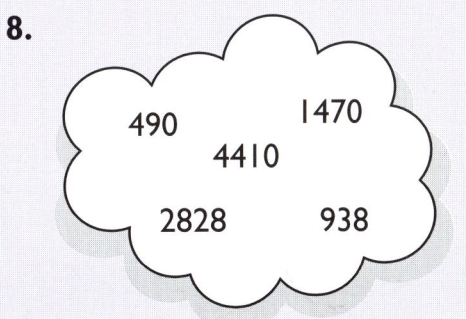

1.
216, 810, 351, 981, 702

2.
1050, 62375, 84525, 600, 725

3.
3315, 2301, 2613, 702, 390

4.
760, 720, 1136, 360, 592

5.
1206, 1530, 828, 360, 1782

6.
2980, 720, 624, 1488, 480

7.
6756, 7500, 7908, 7848, 1440

8.
490, 1470, 4410, 2828, 938

Pick two numbers from a set. Is the highest common factor the same as for the whole set? Try different pairs.

Code squares

Work out what number each letter stands for.

Read rows from left to right and columns from top to bottom.

a	−	b	−	c	8
−		+		+	
c	+	c	+	c	12
−		−		+	
b	+	a	−	b	17

8   −8   13

e	+	f	+	e	31
−		+		+	
d	−	d	+	f	13
+		+		−	
d	−	e	+	f	16

9   34   9

Design your own code square.

46